NET NEEDLE

Robert Adamson was born in Sydney in 1943 and grew up in Neutral Bay and on the Hawkesbury River, New South Wales, Australia. During a tumultuous youth, he found his way to poetry, and in the five decades since he has produced 20 books of poetry and three books of prose. From 1970 to 1985 he was the driving force behind Australia's *New Poetry* magazine, and in 1987, with Juno Gemes, he established Paper Bark Press, for two decades one of Australia's leading poetry publishers. He was the inaugural CAL chair of poetry at UTS (University of Technology, Sydney) in 2011-14. He has won many major Australian poetry awards, including the Christopher Brennan Prize for lifetime achievement, the Patrick White Award, and *The Age* Book of the Year Award for *The Goldfinches of Baghdad* (Flood Editions, 2006), and The Victorian Premier's Poetry Award for *The Golden Bird* (Black Inc, 2009). He has published three books in Britain with Bloodaxe: *Reading the River: Selected Poems* (2004), *The Kingfisher's Soul* (2009) and *Net Needle* (2016).

ROBERT ADAMSON

NET NEEDLE

BLOODAXE BOOKS

ISBN: 978 1 78037 301 0

This edition first published 2016 by
Bloodaxe Books Ltd,
Eastburn,
South Park,
Hexham,
Northumberland NE46 1BS.

First published in 2015 in the US by Flood Editions
and in Australia by Black Inc.

www.bloodaxebooks.com
For further information about Bloodaxe titles
please visit our website or write to
the above address for a catalogue.

Supported using public funding by
ARTS COUNCIL
ENGLAND

Cover design: Neil Astley & Pamela Robertson-Pearce.

Printed in Great Britain by Bell & Bain Limited, Glasgow, Scotland, on
acid-free paper sourced from mills with FSC chain of custody certification.

for Juno

heart's needle, soul's compass

ACKNOWLEDGEMENTS

This book was completed during my three-year appointment as Chair of Poetry at the University of Technology, Sydney (2011-14), and was first published in 2015 in the US by Flood Editions and in Australia by Black Inc.

Versions of these poems have appeared in the following publications: *The Age, The Australian, Australian Book Review, Australian Poetry Journal, Crickey, Eureka Street, HEAT, Jacket, Newswrite, The Sydney Morning Herald, The Red Room Company's The Poetry Object*, and *The Times Literary Supplement*; as well as in *The Best Australian Poems* (Black Inc) 2012, 2013, and 2014. 'Via Negativa, The Divine Dark' won the Blake Poetry Prize in 2011 and appeared in the accompanying catalogue. A chapbook, *Empty Your Eyes* (Vagabond Press, 2013), included eleven of these poems. *Shark-Net Seahorses of Balmoral: A Harbour Memoir*, an artist's book limited to 36 copies, included 12 others along with 21 linocuts by Peter Kingston.

CONTENTS

All the stream that's roaring by
Came out of a needle's eye;
Things unborn, things that are gone,
From needle's eye still goad it on.

WILLIAM BUTLER YEATS

PART ONE

Listening to Cuckoos

Two unchanging notes; to us, words – always those high
elongated notes. Red-eyed koels with feathered earmuffs,

downward-ending notes that pour through a falling of night
coming over the distances, words that don't change.

The two notes remain, a split phrase, two words
meaning, not exactly a self – not quite, the first day of spring.

The moment of utterance, candour becomes
the piercing, whistled syllables. Penetrating the dark green

of twilight, the storm birds call, two notes, two words,
and cackle in the broken-egged dawn, in the echoing light.

Summer

(after Georg Trakl)

A pallid cuckoo calls in a loop
more insistently as afternoon fades.

In garden beds humid air
clings to the stalks of poppies.

Mosquitoes rise from layers
of leaves under grapevines.

A blue shirt sticks to your back
as you climb the ladder.

Thunder rattles a fishing boat's
canopy in the dry dock.

The storm silences crickets
chirruping under the mangroves.

Turbulence has passed.
A candle lights our dark room.

Outside, calm, a starless night –
then the flame is extinguished,

pinched between a finger
and thumb. In the eaves, at nest,

swallows rustle. You believe
the swallows glow in the dark.

Light daubs our skin with shapes –
the crushed petals of red poppies.

Garden Poem
(for Juno)

Sunlight scatters wild bees across a blanket
of flowering lavender. The garden

grows, visibly, in one morning –
native grasses push up, tough and lovely

as your angel's trumpets. At midday
the weather, with bushfire breath, walks about

talking to itself. A paper wasp zooms
above smooth river pebbles. In the trees

possums lie flat on leafy branches to cool off,
the cats notice, then fall back to sleep.

This day has taken our lives to arrive.
Afternoon swings open, although

the mechanics of the sun require
the moon's white oil. Daylight fades to twilight

streaking bottlebrush flowers with shade,
a breeze clatters in the green bamboo and shakes

its lank hair. At dinnertime, the French doors present us
with a slice of night, shining clear –

a Naples yellow moon outlines the ridges
of the mountains – all this, neatly laid out

on the dining room table
across patches of moonlight.

Dorothy Wordsworth

Wisps of smoke, lamplight on manuscripts.
Pages fanned across an oak stool.
The hearth absorbs the stain of living.

A window frames stars. He is asleep,
Stirs because I opened the curtains.
The moon traveled across the star-flecked dark

Out of sight almost an hour ago.
I want to sketch time into some new shape
And hold it in my hands.

Our house, anchored to the present: night
Unfolds towards dawn, as scrawled letters in a flock
Migrate from between finger and thumb

To the page, eye to mind. I watch
The hour's hand as it smears my face with shadow.
The lake smokes, an owl works strips

Of flesh from a claw-full of bone and fur.
The moment's a sentence, condensed into our life.
A journal of twisted but hopeful thought.

Manuscript's wings brush against
A turning hand. A frog on the back step sings, clock,
What o'clock. Calligraphic knots,

Chaffed fingers, ink under fingernails.
Sight's locked in the mind's cupboard, burning.

Henning Brand's *phosphorus* – cold fire
In a bottle – shake till time breaks on a surface;
Midnight, cotton flowers bloom in the rag-moth's head.

Via Negativa, The Divine Dark

1 *A Poem without Birds*

> My Worthiness is all my Doubt
> EMILY DICKINSON

This morning the tree-ferns woke and opened out
as sunlight dispersed a thick mist –
      morning in a memory incised

with old phrases, mouthing
words then uttering a sentence with an unfinished
      breath. Banana trees rustle,

a first breeze arrives, bringing the perfumes
of the ebb; watermarks down on the mudflats begin
      to disappear.

Morning turns its back on the sun;
gradually, night arrives. In the skylight,
stars appear through the smoke screen from a burn-off,
      brilliant pinholes.

Stars are clustered trees, hung in the night sky.

Whose body, whose eyes? Look
up into the heavens: the problem of suffering
expands forever – dust and light again,
      maybe time, if it exists.

On the table a cicada, flecked with flour,
opening its dry cellophane wings.

The cat flies across polished space illuminated by the
kitchen's energy-saving light bulb,
      a Philips 'Genie'.

Life like a dirty wind blowing straight
through a snowy head, cat eyes, tint of fur, a rustling.
          Praise life   with broken words.

2 *A Preliminary Sketch*

What I see not, I better see
EMILY DICKINSON

An old shack by the river, deserted for years now,
haunted by mesh nets and anchor rope,

wild apple trees grow out the back.
A charcoal sketch of this scene unfurls before me

on a sheet of mist, I push aside tough vines of
morning glory and then walk on, into the drawing.

It's difficult to move in this landscape,
and I have forgotten the names of most flora and fauna.

Cross-hatched charcoal enfolds me
and I become a part of the subject matter, my shape

drawn carefully, sharp and figurative.
However, precision no longer interests me:

my attention is focused by smudges, the forms
grown vague – just fifty years ago

a country of sandstone and gums, a second ago
ferns and hardship. The heavy tidal swings

roll corks and drown fish caught by their gills
in the smothering mesh. In the distance bushfire

writes its killer lines – orange loops, burning serifs
spill over the sandstone escarpments.

I fished these tides when I was young
and abstract – what rubbed off, what idea sunk home?

I rejected the lessons and feared my mother's God,
the Christ I couldn't believe in. The friends

in those days, the ones I loved, are now drawn
beside me in the margins. The kirk

we attended appears, the place where the minister
refused tell me exactly what a soul might be –

although mine, come Judgment Day,
would be flung into Hell, along with the others

who weren't chosen. The Presbyterian soul
is not mysterious, rather it's something we were

lumped with. Now I rise from the sketch,
my face smeared with ink from years of sinning –

back on the river, my boat plows through fog.
I'm looking hard. What form, shape, or song

might represent a soul? What words, paint, or mud
resemble such an intangible glow?

A stain of mist hangs above a black-butt,
brushed by the wings of a grey-headed flying fox.

Colonial Whaler

As a boy, he watched a spear
made of bone fly underwater
to land a crab efficaciously
before his mother's eyes –

its sandy claw, loose in the air,
a parrot-snap, the mouth-flaps
clicking open, shut.
He wanted to gaff

a bladder fish from the Pacific
for its pearl-sized eggs
black as Beluga caviar.
Maybe only the young whaler

longed for those sleek
handmade weapons:
towards the end he took up
an industrial harpoon, serrated,

designed to sink and grip, sharper,
harder than the black-edged beak
of a jet-propelled squid –
the lost navigator's pen and ink.

Net Makers

They stitched their lives into my days,
Blue's Point fishermen, with a smoke
stuck to their bottom lips, bodies bent

forward, inspecting a haul-net's wing
draped from a clothes line. Their hands
darting through mesh, holding bone

net needles, maybe a special half-needle
carved from tortoise shell. Their fingers,
browned by clusters of freckles

and tobacco tar, slippery with speed –
they wove everything they knew
into the mesh, along with the love they had,

or had lost, or maybe not needed.
During my school holidays I watched them
and came to love this craft

of mending, in our backyard by the harbour,
surrounded by copper tubs brimming
with tanning soup brewed from

bloodwood and wild-apple bark.
These men could cut the heart clean
from a fish with a swipe of a fillet knife

and fill buckets with gut flecked
with the iridescent backs of flies
as it fermented into liquid fertiliser.

I'd water my father's beds of vegetables,
rows of silverbeet, a fence of butterbeans.
In the last of the sun, I'd watch

our peacock spread its fan; the hose
sprayed water from a water tank, house high
fed by gravity.

PART TWO

Heaving the Rope

A ferry kisses the wharf –
engine rumble, shudder,
and prop-churn stir
the tide to white foam.
A deck hand makes a line
then heaves his rope,
lassos a bollard.
There's a golden codger
fishing for blackfish,
his long rod and float,
green weed for bait.
The local boys, wharf rats
who fish all hours.
A businessman in bright
pinstripes walks
the gangplank. Boys
at Manly, diving from
pylons for silver coins,
girls off to Luna Park
or to school on the other
shore. The ferry's
deckie ropes in the life
of the harbour – his
world framed by seagulls
and Southerly busters –
when he heaves the rope.

Chowder Bay

The nights at Chowder Bay were illegible.
Out from the wharf, the bottom
dropped off into a deep valley.
Past squid and circling yellowtail,
ribbonfish hovered in the water column,
swimming vertically, like chrome-plated
seahorses. In the darkness
before dawn a blanket of mist
would float across the tide –
when the sun rose, it seemed a pale hole
in morning's roof. Our baits
became bleached and tough,
the wharf gradually disappeared in fog.
Cold air cramped our fingers.
Around 9 a.m. the white haze
lifted – then macaws from Taronga Zoo
flew in, flaring with reds
and blues. They'd pull green curtains
apart and take centre stage,
exotic escapees, then fly to our side
of the bay. We watched as their beaks
flashed in sun, red-tipped question marks
punctuating empty branches of jacaranda trees.

The Green Flash

One day my mother took me for a walk
across Sydney Harbour Bridge.
When we reached the other side
I became fed up and threw
a tantrum, so she ushered me
into the 'Pylon Lookout'. We climbed
stairs up into a room that grabbed
attention with model Spitfires,
Lancaster bombers suspended
in the air, photos of submarines,
Catalina flying boats at Rose Bay.
There was a café, where mum bought
my first Devonshire tea.
Afterwards, we climbed a ladder
with rusty rungs, and reaching the top,
looked out across the harbour:
cats pranced along the pylon wall, nothing
between them and ground below,
others rode a miniature carousel.
There seemed to be dozens of them –
'Mrs Rentoul's famous white cats.'
This was the spot my father took
my mother on their first date; he always
knew how to impress people.
I remember the long walk
to Blues Point where my grandfather
lived back then. Many decades later,
he moved to the Hawkesbury –
'fish around Sydney became very scarce'.
He was in his late nineties when I asked him
where he set his nets in those days:
'I'd shoot them right under the Bridge –
this was before they built it – there'd be boxes
of them, blackfish, mullet, bream.'

The Wintergarden

We'd walk to the Saturday matinee,
my little brother dressed as an Indian chief,
chook feathers for a headdress
and a green bamboo bow and arrow
for the fancy dress prize.

We loaded up with bullets,
honeycomb and sherbet cones,
our shirts sticky in the heat –
we walked around the bay in a blaze
of midday sun, the Wintergarden

our shelter from stinking weather.
Straight through its open doors
into the heart of America:
Movietone newsreels – O that smooth
well-spoken voice as it described

a hell overseas, 'Korea Heroes:
Aussies Home From Prison Camps' –
or a serious fairytale, the Coronation
of Elizabeth II, 'one last moment of glory'
the tone of authority. We knew

next week Rocket Man would fly again,
and Mr Magoo wisecrack
from the side of his mouth.
At the Wintergarden before each show,
as they rolled the shutters up,

we'd smell the ozone from the bay
as it washed over us, then pulley chains
clattered as we settled in, feathers
alive with expectation – every Saturday,
a new world would begin.

The River Caves

We were keen young cubs, members
of Third Mosman Bay Sea Scouts,
twelve years old and full
of excitement, collecting donations
for the clubhouse charity.
On bob-a-job week we walked
up and down steep streets
around the harbour, mowing
lawns, raking leaves, taking
on any work we were offered.
A woman asked us to remove
a huge white carp from one
of her garden ponds:
dead for a week, its smell clung
to our uniforms all day –
she had a mansion with a
suburban jungle surrounding it.
One Saturday morning
we ended up at Luna Park,
wandered in, and came across
the River Caves – a ride
that carried us in brightly
painted boats through dark
tunnels to illuminated caverns.
By the time we entered
the second cave we were looking
for trouble. The next cave
was an artificial South Pole,
with ice and hundreds of penguins.
I jumped out first
and the others followed. Our boat
moved on so fast it left us
stranded. We heard the next one
coming, and, not to be caught,

I told my friends to 'freeze' – as if
we were models of cubs in a landscape,
the frozen Sea Scouts of the River Caves.

The Sydney Stadium

Sydney Stadium's stage revolved slowly, the fighters
and artists had to walk down the aisle to get to it.

I heard mention of the Stadium one night
when my father came home late, talking
about a big event. Jimmy Carruthers
was to fight Bobby Sinn, an aboriginal
warrior from Brisbane; the press
had named him the Bulimba Bull Ant,
our next champion. Back then the match
was a big deal but now who can recall
the outcome? I remember through
a newspaper photograph of the Stadium.

I applied for work at Rushcutters Bay;
my mother wasn't keen because
it was across the Bridge, but I landed a job.
Gradually I got to know the Stadium by selling
programs at the gates. My first concert
was Little Richard, the wildest rocker
to visit Sydney that year. As the crowd grew,
I sold stacks of booklets with Richard's photo
on the cover and made heaps.

Halfway through the show, I was allowed
to watch from the back, though couldn't see over
the heads of a gang of rockers, all I heard was
screaming and loud noise. I rode my bike
home that night across the Bridge,
a southerly whistling through steel girders.

A year later I returned, as a paying
customer this time. My girlfriend
had dumped me, and Johnnie Ray cut loose
with 'I'll Never Fall in Love Again'.

I was with him all the way, in the middle
of his song 'Cry' he cracked up and
tears fell down his face. Of them all,
I most remember Judy Garland, who'd been
hounded by the local press – she sang
a couple of songs, stopped the orchestra,
sat on the edge of the stage, took a drink and said:
'Well, this is what you've all come to see, isn't it.'

The Shark-Net Seahorses of Balmoral

The swimmers changed into their day clothes
and left the beach to the cleaner, a man
with a spike and rake. Night came and went.
The fishing boy walked onto the sand alone.
At dawn the sky beyond the Heads
flared into sheets of light, as if bombs were
exploding on some distant island. Thunder
was absent and silence wasn't reassuring.
He was in tune with details of the beach,
the calm above yellow sand – a bay with water

clear as white spirit – blue-ringed octopus,
sepia kelp with drifting sharkskin leaves.
Some mornings penguins would swim in and dive
for slender garfish, surface, then bob and shake
their turquoise heads. Below the scattering
school of gar, whiting cruised for worms.
The beach was the boy's world, on the ebb
he'd collect stranded starfish and throw them back:
first the locals with long spindle-legs, then squat
comic stars, dark-red aliens from Manly.

He loved an underwater fence, a shark net,
hung from a steel cable strung across the bay
from the Island to its anchor embedded
in the wall of a concrete stormwater outlet.
He'd spit into his goggles and adjust a snorkel,
then float across an inverted world: stingrays were
birds of prey – the prawns, crabs, and lobsters,
insects of the eelgrass and the rocks.
The shark net was a hanging garden under the tide,
beaded seaweed, marine-fern, black periwinkles.

The boy looked for his favorite creatures, seahorses:
they'd ride the water column in single file
and look through the net's squares of wire mesh.
It was a protection zone, the other side,
beyond the pale. The mottled seahorses
could see into a cave where a groper lived,
and sensed somehow it couldn't get through the net.
Hovering there in clear sight of the old fish
they'd click and buck, as if they knew how to tease
the hungry, blue-eyed predator.

The Phantom

My father was a fisherman who made
his own nets and he'd use lengths
of horsehair for the crab snares.

On weekdays, he drove his horse
and cart to the Fisherman's Co-Op;
Saturdays, he'd hitch up

a sulky and take me to Paddy's
Markets. It seemed he was always
working, except when

he drank at the Oaks Hotel.
He relaxed by reading paperback
Westerns, unless a new edition of

The Phantom had been released –
then he'd lay on the floor
and read it right through; we weren't

allowed to interrupt, if we did
it meant trouble. Our mother
would say, leave your father alone,

can't you see he's reading his Phantom.
The years went by and I wrote
many books, none of which he read.

Whenever we spoke, it was
about cars or fishing. He came
to see our new place on the Hawkesbury,

walked into my study – the walls
stacked with books and paintings –
looked about and considered

things, his eye fixed on a print,
a pop art version of the Phantom,
then in a conspiratorial tone, he said,
'There he is.'

MV Anytime

The deep greens of Middle Harbour,
our boat moving smoothly across
a glossy surface. The day spread
before us as we motor upstream. Pete's dog,
Denton sits on the stern taking it in,
shooting the breeze. We hear the sound
of a wind coming across the tide –
a gale, turbulent, black, and fast.
We lunge as the first gust hits,
whistles its thick tune, waves become
rusty-coloured and break across
the bow, a blast of water lashes
our faces. We decide to push onwards,
waves and the wind driving
into the side of the boat, white water
crashing around us. Denton braces himself
at the stern and stands his ground,
fixed to the deck. Waves
are full of wind, towering above the deck
and crashing down – how
can a day turn upside down without
warning? Denton becomes
our symbol, evidence of staying power,
we look to him as gusts whip their
threads of salt across our faces.
The motor strains and a valve rattles. Denton
sits tuned by instinct to stand there
and ride out the fury of invisible breath.

Sugarloaf Bay, Middle Harbour

Marcia Hathaway, aged 32, was fatally attacked by a bull
shark, on January 28th, 1963. She was wading Sugarloaf Bay
in Middle Harbour.

I fished here for leatherjackets,
and the summer whiting –
in late winter a John Dory might drift
slowly through shallows
stalking angelfish. On the shore

lantana teemed with ticks;
kookaburras swooped for snakes,
sacred kingfishers aimed for whitebait.
On the slopes, fine houses
with swimming pools.

I'd overturn rocks on the shore
searching for pink nippers.
One day I watched a dollarbird tumble
down the sky and almost
hit the surface of the tide.

There were veils of barbecue smoke
smelling of sausages and onions
that drifted from the stern
of a Halversen cruiser at anchor;
children laughed and dogs barked in sunlight.

The green water was deep,
days were mostly blue – when it rained,
the orange domes of man-o'-war
jellyfish would break
the surface as they sailed along.

On windless mornings, the bay
stretched tight, a glass drum,
as if waiting for the vibration of an
unknown force, some dark fin that might cut
a pathway to civilisation.

The Long Bay Debating Society

I spent my twenty-first in Long Bay Penitentiary
Each day in the front yards
We paced up and down
At night I read novels
And the poetry of Percy Shelley
Sometimes an education officer
Would turn up and ask
What are you going to do with your future?
I'd tell him I wanted to be a poet
He would shake his head
And comment I was being insolent
After weeks I convinced him
We wanted to start a debating team
There were plenty of crims
Who would join up
It took a month to convince the Governor
Finally the authorities agreed
We could form debating society
Things went well and we attended library
And researched our topics
Then came the day a team
From the outer agreed to come inside
And conduct a debate with us
However there was a condition
The Governor would chose the topic
Eventually the prison librarian
Ceremoniously handed us the Governor's note
(it was the summer of 1964) our topic
'Is the Sydney Opera House Really Necessary?'

The Coriander Fields of Long Bay Penitentiary

Serving two years hard;
my thoughts – sweet
as torn basil, or tinged
with broken roots
of coriander – soothe
fragmented fears.

When the mind's blank
I cultivate musky
persimmons, ideas
flutter, cabbage moths –
one with a lopsided wing
spins in circles.

I swallow, nothing's
left of my pride –
the prison doctor stitched
my cut wrists
without anaesthetic,
his idea of punishment.

Laying with a blanket
on the bed-board,
I think of poppy fields
in the high country of Tasmania,
sun-splotched red blooms
loaded with seed,

their hairy stalks raked
by a wind from Antarctica;
here in my black slot,
an imaginary whiff
of opium mingles with
the bitter aftertaste of iodine.

PART THREE

Internal Weather, for Randolph Stow

I dwell in this bone-cave   rocking cup of skull
histories   constantly   re-writing themselves   weave

'brain waves' with drift   out from the body's net
a fatty backwash   veins of grainy information

blood cells   push into the white country
in multiples of ten   you know nothing's lost

we remembered   how sand   streamed in syllables
lines breaking into phrases   static sparks   weather breaks

rain-splattered paper   torn memories   the flicker
as sparks ping against blue tats   a pink tongue   so alive

touching porcelain   internal canals   the gush
woven nests   waves of fine hair   fragments of shells

Cannot evaporate   can't die down   we live
at the world's expense   devouring   pale afterimages

with a bad weather eye   the serif-tails
chalk up   fine stainless blades   score the walls of arteries

a typewriter of bones   tapping   Morse on the spine's
fretwork   the philosopher   a machine   ticking out days

skidding down aisles in the supermalls   I stand here
in a column of breath   mixed with fine dust from red dirt

polishing fingernails   hair combed   dressed to
cast the same net   over leagues of broken weather

Francis Webb at Ball's Head

Sandstone dust swirled into the westerly,
settled on the tide off Ball's Head – a whale
rose from its rock, slid into Berrys Bay,
then moved off towards deeper water.
Francis watched the artist who carved it
'brush death from his wits' again.
The windy sky stretched above him

and his interlocutor, the sun, flared
on windscreens of cars cruising the road
near the council fence in need of paint.
Francis knew time as a whirlpool.
He saw the baker's horse he loved, swishing
its tail, flies on its back, the oily harness.
A straightjacket and regimental clock

swung through the night of his dream,
along with the animals from tidal dreaming.
He watched the carcass of the old horse
overrun by a group of taunting boys
pulling its black tail and dusty mane.
In his mind language gathered
its storm clouds, lightning-carved

grooves in the sandstone; waves broke
and spilled their sparks on oily rocks.
Seagull shit streaked the coal wharf;
white flakes on pylons reflected tug-light.
Francis ran fingers across the whale's groves.
Night, hard night. A few pence, homeless
young men around a fire on the shore

with bacon-bone soup. Pinchgut Island.
The moon shone, an escaped convict
who swam the harbour, lit up the wings
of flying foxes and sea mullet in mid leap –
channels, lead lines, corks and the difference.
The tide full and whitebait hatched.
The Head is alive.

Poem Beginning with a Line from William Blake

I was in a Printing house in Hell & saw the method in which
knowledge is transmitted from generation to generation.

On the first floor a rainbow bee-eater
was being handfed blue wasps by an apiarist,
his head draped in alphabets of lace.

On the second floor a chef prepared
choux pastry, piping unpunctuated duck liver
into his chocolate éclairs.

On the third floor bookbinders were bent over tables,
though instead of the usual dovetail joints
drove screws into stanzas of poetry.

Whose eyes did I look through on the fourth floor?
Only an owl could process the illegible scenes
behind those doors of flesh –

The fifth floor was a place for grinding down bones
for bone-black ink, pulverised from
the carbonised skulls of hummingbirds.

The sixth floor was a rocky paddock of spinifex grass
where an expedition of ornithologists had created
a semblance of darkness for night parrots.

On the seventh level was a futuristic installation
with recorded voice repeating: 'The bees have never
existed, forget the myth of honey.'

On the eighth floor was a display case
exhibiting a branch of twisted amber
embedded in its tip, the transparent imprint of a tiny wing.

I looked for the word trauma in the eyes
of strangers who might hold my gaze, but people growled
and turned their heads away.

Ballad of the Word *Trauma*

The idea of 'massive road trauma' drifts
in a hospital atmosphere, a voice by the side of the bed
whispers: 'the field opens to music.'

This voice holds your soul within its cage
of bones, radiates affection, received by your skin's
soft parachute. Then a tongue

rears up to speak into the silence,
memory turns and blocks the door of sleep,
draws out temper into a wire that streams

names of lost relatives. Trauma can't be
contained in particular shapes, it eventually becomes
abstract fire, power, thought, light –

at other times it broods like a mullet outside
in the rank smokehouse. Trauma becomes a wall
of skin and bone, a barricade of flesh

proving human arms stroking air are not wings.
A brushtail's touch, fanned by a cry under
the shadow of an owl-shaped drone

passing over broken strings, tangled across
the lyrebird's quarterdeck, where its tail's reflection
on a lake is crazed by glowing twigs –

embers spit and hiss on the surface.
A human rustles in the undergrowth, a marsupial
moves through the dark until its cough

becomes a rattle. Trauma the infection
carried on the breath of the man who repeats his orders:
'At ease, attention, pull yourself together.'

After Shelley's *Satan Broken Loose*

He stood before the Final Judgment, pupils
dilated from a tab of GHB and shots of white rum,
wings shaking, looking a mess, hands raw,
his feet bare. The Father and the Son knew
this angel before them was first of things to come.

Satan had unchained himself from the sky:
he ranged back and forth across the world
with his crew of demons on an Airbus 777.
Before this angel could spin his cryptic lie
a thrilling sound of dark wings taking flight
was heard in heaven – then the lights went out.

The Sibyl's Avenue

Lovers strolled in a city park
Under branches of finely etched trees.
Ample sun leaked down the sky
As autumn oak leaves fell

Scattering fragments of calligraphy.
All this, locked away when a bell
Rings. Memory leaks, touching sunlight;
Though with a kind of ease

My hand draws back –
The sky isn't blue it's abstract.
Those who walk this cracked
Avenue do so to pay the rent in paradise.

No takers, no shared accom.
A man sells methadone twice
Diluted at his garish mobile bar.
The burbling exhaust

Of his fuel, cotton oil, curdles the air;
Bent hotdogs talk to strangers.
Still, the oak trees flower above us,
A canopy of lust – look over there,

The sparrows chitter, just far
Enough away from a cat, who chitters back.
This is to let you know I'll still be here,
As time repeats its fact.

The Midnight Zoo

(for Sonya Hartnett)

A bronze pigeon fans the humid air.
I follow its sleek calligraphy,
dancing, calling you back.
Under the colonial clock,
a Malvern Star, its front wheel
an echidna of broken spokes.
All night neon flickers
and says you know the way
as a snow leopard paws
the ground – forget the pigeon
becoming part of the bronze
distance. News from an unending
war breaks onto the airwaves,
it's Martha Gellhorn, correspondent,
attacking her typewriter.
We need space without time.
A pelican's beak-clack
by a lyrebird. The kids fall apart.
Parking meters tick away
in freshly enameled metal jackets
on the verge of ignition.
The red glow and blue lights of the
City across the harbour –
or the Bridge pulsing green
and solemnly playing itself. Seagulls
breakfast on bogong moths
and black commas. Forget the warnings,
though don't leave your place,
this isn't official history anymore.

Michael Dransfield in Tasmania

A lagoon reflects low sky:
clouds seen are clouds
as seen – words open
their shells in his brain.
We study a drawing
of Emma's night parrot.
Imagination shifts,
fails us on the slope.
Campfire flares to feathers,
a parrot-green light
for the rescue party.
He patched up words
and paper in a loft, here
extinction's ornithologists
thrive on the poorly
written histories.
The embers are scales
covering the legs,
feet adapted for ground
with slightly upturned
claws. Just after dawn
he swings a metaphor
to make the tea. The tent's
gone stiff with frost,
on the floor his maps
await a torturer's nib:
ink's dark, although
not quite indelible, lines
begin to unravel.
Clocks and theories
slash leaves, clip wings
in remnant wilderness.
At Rushy Lagoon, birds
bow and call the light –

James McAuley wrote
sharp lyrics here. He walked
around the shore,
chanting: 'the broken
trust, the litter and the stink'.
Mount Ossa's dolerite
candlesticks can't flicker
on a coast that's never clear.

Francis Thompson

(1859–1907)

He slept by the Thames
in newspaper, a makeshift

blanket, fevered talk.
Opium pipe, 'Black Drops'.

How much did it cost
for his pencil to move

across paper? At dawn
a fox limped by, coughed up

a sparrow at his feet.
Francis addressed envelopes

in a curved hand
to enfold his poems,

posting them off
from Charing Cross –

When they appeared in print
he'd worry about his best lines.

A century later, I read
The Hound of Heaven

by a river in New South Wales
and heard a dark chuckle

before his 'running laughter' –
Attention shifts, revelation grips.

The Confessions

(after Saint Augustine)

When my first love, Una,
was torn from my side
it crushed my heart.

We sent her back to Africa –
an obstacle to marriage
and advancement in Rome.

When she left, my diseased
soul fluttered above
my mother's glowing head.

Months passed. News
arrived – Una vowed she'd
never love another man.

Our son lived with me
inside the gates, grew up
without the sanction of wedlock.

Una lived alone
and drank wild honey
in attempts to ease the pain.

There'd be no healing;
absence remained a wound,
although, a slave to lust, I took

a mistress; through long days
and streaky nights
my raw side festered.

Meanwhile, I was sinning
more and more – fully aware,
no matter what, there'd be no cure –

Empty Your Eyes

(after Pierre Reverdy)

The suffering has ended. Empty your eyes, a new era begins. Heads, once out of line, have fallen. People call from windows. Surrounded by laughter becoming noise, others call up to the windows. Animals never seen before come out from the alleys. There are broad-faced women with broad accents walking pavements, talking freely, their faces lit up, their hair undone. Sunlight, trumpets, and pianos are playing boogie. Emboldened, people smile in public places. The intact houses blink, doors swing open and somehow smile back to other houses. The banal parade floats above the ash of iron filings. A mother with a blue apron that frames her baby, cheers at random, another child by her side trembles, astonished and fearful. There's an apparition of an angel, timid and adrift in the midst of life, while rustling people gather in the square. Foreigners pass by in a group, singing under bright umbrellas, their lyrics sleek and empty. A grandfather goes about extinguishing street lamps against the coming radiance. A jazz dancer leaps out from her suitcase with an answer nobody can understand. A policeman rides his one-wheeled bike, his thighs swollen against black leggings. He circles the stragglers, until a spotlight picks up his problem. The circus of shadows moves through the jumping city as rackets break their own strings. On the far ramparts, a boy with a thousand dreams cries because he feels he is ugly.

Sensation

(after Rimbaud)

One morning in summer
I'll go down some lane,
as my feet flatten the sand

lantana will prick my arms.
I might enter a dream
where a cool breeze will brush
my tangled hair.

I'll be a clever vagrant
and continue to wander
as the dream repeats itself.

I'll know exactly
what a soul means –
as mine will be filled
to the brim with love.

When I wake my mind
will be empty, then without
a thought in my head, I'll smile
and have no need to speak.

PART FOUR

A Proper Burial

The other night outside our house an owlet nightjar swooped down onto the road after a moth. It bought to mind an encounter last Christmas, with a pair of tawny frogmouths. Driving on the highway, alongside the Hawkesbury River, I noticed what seemed to be an injured bird. I pulled over and walked back to where the bird was lying and found a tawny frogmouth had been killed on the road. I picked up its limp body and carried it to the side of the highway, where I discovered another frogmouth, dead in a scattering of leaves. I looked around and there was a young aboriginal girl standing behind me. She was wearing a white dress and seemed rather shy. I have lived here for most of my life, but I had never met or even seen her before, so I wondered where she came from. She held out a bag and said, 'I will take them away for a proper burial.' I asked her, 'What happened here?' 'All the cars kept going. Some ran over one of the already dead birds. You are the only one who stopped.' She went on to explain the female frogmouth was the first hit, then the male flew down to the side of his mate, trying to help somehow. As the girl watched, the second frogmouth was also run down by a car coming the other way. The girl had walked out onto the highway and picked up one of the birds and placed it on a bed of gum leaves by the side of the road. Then she had gone to get a bag to carry them, which is when I turned up. We knelt on the leaves and carefully placed both frogmouths into the used onion bag. When it was done, the girl stood up with the bag in her hand, then without comment walked off, heading for Mooney Point Road. I was left standing there by the paperbarks, shaken. It had been an upsetting experience, but somehow the girl made it easier to take. I went home with the milk I had gone out to buy in the first place. Our house was full of people, family and friends gathered for Christmas. I tried to tell my wife what happened, though it felt so out of context, a scene from another dimension. I went into my study, closed the door, and sat there going over things. Frogmouths are closer to nightjars than owls and related to both species; they're nocturnal hunters and so usually sleep by day. But these two had been run down in broad daylight. This episode, though that's hardly the right word, has never left my mind.

The Easterly

An easterly breeze arrives and within an hour strengthens into a gale that whips the surface of the river. Fishing boats power back to moorings, their hulls thump as they hit each wave. Before outboard motors, the fishermen had a saying: 'When there's no wind row out on the high, if it looks like a blow, don't go.' Advice for mesh-netters. Somewhere around Easter, the luderick come on the bite; they are vegetarians and seek out filamentous algae. I look for them in certain spots until I see their distinctive shapes, olive-green bodies with dark tiger stripes across their backs. They hover between bridge pylons and graze on strands of weed, fine as green hair, or what's left of it, after the surgeonfish have snipped away a feed. I row home at night through the calm air, dipping the oars – reflected stars flash on the blades, glowing with phosphorescence from Fukushima.

After the Deluge

After torrential rain the mountains glisten. On the sandstone escarpments orange flakes of iron ore rust in the sun. The river turns a dirty milk from the run-off. When the tide comes up from Broken Bay, a translucent layer of salt water floats on the top of the fresh from the rain. Powerful eddies form and draw shoals of mullet into spiraling pockets of tide. Mulloway, wolves of the river, circle these trapped schools of fish, picking off the stragglers with precision teamwork. After dusk in the still air, a full moon reflects across the river as it moves between the mountains – a stream of mercury. Above the swirling mullet, a pair of white-shouldered sea eagles swing into avoidance manoeuvres and bark at the friarbirds who mob them. Today around dusk I watched as a letter-winged kite hovered above the tide: stationed neatly in the air, it held this position for five minutes before deciding not to swoop.

The Whiting

One winter afternoon I went fishing, and around dusk caught a nice one. For a whiting it was quite large, fairly lean yet thick with roe; this abundance of eggs had stretched the skin, and its belly was almost transparent. The fish had swallowed my hook – traumatised, there was no point releasing it back into the wild, so I found myself killing my catch by cutting its throat. Scaled and cleaned the fish right there on the beach. As I removed its gut, I noticed without the orange roe there wasn't much flesh on the body, making it too difficult to slice into fillets. I took the whiting home and cooked it whole. There were two of us for dinner, so we picked what little flesh there was from the bones, hardly enough to satisfy, but sweet. Later on we made a fire in the grate. After a while a sleek, familiar shadow slid into the lounge room. I couldn't make out what kind of animal it was until I realised there was something of the whiting in its demeanour. As I stared the cat seemed to resemble the fish, while retaining its feline body shape. Then the animal came up to the lounge chair, rubbed itself against my leg and started to purr loudly. Although we had eaten the whiting, the presence of the fish managed to shine through this odd creature – the spirit of the whiting was alive in our new pet. A visiting friend bent over to pat the strange cat. 'Be careful,' I said, 'can't you see the poor animal is still recovering from that wound in its belly?'

Wombats

Driving through Kangaroo Valley
I glimpsed a low-slung animal
in the headlights. Recognising
a wombat, I pulled over: fog
lifted its gauze; a clump of fern
moved apart; another animal
trundled out, then a third
came into view, larger this time,
with darker colouring.
All three moved in a rough circle.
I turned off the headlights
and squinted through the glow
of parking lights – too dim to see –
then grabbed a torch and rolled
the window down. Frogs pumped
deep in the undergrowth, nightjars
passed along their liquid calls –
in the middle of the highway wombats
were doing the double shuffle.

The Great Auk

(for Charles Buckmaster)

Birding in Boulder with Merrill, the Rockies
behind us as we walked by Walden Ponds
listening for warblers. We talked about
great auks: evidently they once
lived throughout the North Atlantic
from Norway, Greenland, Iceland, right
down to the Gulf of St Lawrence. There were
rumours of great auks in Ireland,
and in our conversation they
came pouring out of Jack
Collom's 'Great Auk' poem into the air
around our heads, though
they were long extinct and unable to fly.
I mentioned that many years ago
there was a poetry journal
called *The Great Auk*, published for a season
or two in Melbourne, edited
by a young poet named
Charles Buckmaster. Once it travelled
to Sydney and charmed the bookshop people
who offered it a sanctuary for
a while. Charles spoke of auk bones
discovered in Massachusetts, fragments put
together by the archaeologist of morning, kingfisher
of poets. Charles wrote for the lost forest
and opened new pages as he
walked the streets of Melbourne,
writing back the great auks, speaking of branches
to sing from; as the growth rings
thickened our lives, he stretched himself imagining
pilchards in massive schools
turning oceans silver with auk food –
auks returning in poems, swimming from the heads
of poets, into the tides of our words.

Carnaby's Cockatoo

A wandering koel whistles
from a thicket of banksia, her eyes
circled with fire, her beak hooked

to dispense killing pecks.
The male answers, his call echoes
distance – scorned by other birds,

attacked by noisy miners.
Yeats' linnets remain as words,
as wings, were never here. Tonight

a flying fox eats warm apple pie
then flaps across dark suburbs
above a thousand swimming pools

with glowing chemicals.
The local apprentices
leave their hot cars up on blocks

and fork out for weekly bus tickets
to a factory's pervasive clock.
Pentecostalists pray to avian spirits

as they imagine cuckoos
flying from tree to thicker tree
into a world of lost chicks.

A pair of Carnaby's come and go
from a stand of melaleucas in a zoo –
they don't suffer noisy miners

and ignore the mystique of koels,
though still mocking them, drawing
from a screech the two infamous notes.

Harsh Song

Afternoon's
pulse,
a feathery
susurration –
half song,
soft
leather
ratchet, or
breath
forced
through
a snake's
throat
across
the roof
of its
raked
mouth –
whispered
sounds,
a smoker's
thick
exhalation –
bowerbirds
in the grape vine.

Death of a Goshawk

White goshawk
Hovering on sunlight and air –
A boy's trigger finger.

The Art of War

Bankers and accountants
jostle along the main street, their
umbrellas twitching spikes.

Night approaches,
its silver arms in tatters and
spaced-out face smeared, broken.

The invaders drop
Kalashnikovs, bunker down
and hit their cell phones.

The ash from their orders
falls on the city's outskirts –
the green thorns of suburban hedges

catch tufts of torn flesh.
The sound of a person suffering
travels across the river –

At dawn the ravens call out,
then appear – to frame the picture.
In a cold stream there's colour,

flowers, below the surface –
ulcerated feet in wet boots,
water swirling around the ankles.

Spinoza

O my soul's friend
just once take

some advice
reach back

to myths of flight
measure

a peregrine falcon's
primary feathers

check semiplumes
for bird mites

then hold
your bearings

the law could
break by daylight

you can't afford
this luxury

after inventing
your new lucidity

tonight
open Ezekiel's gates

travel by light
shooting

through veins
and gelatinous

floating lenses
the packed neurons

composing
the optic nerves

of a peregrine's
four-dimensional sight